SEAN OF THE SOUTH

SOUTH

VOLUME II

SEAN DIETRICH

ISBN-13: 978-1519433855
ISBN-10: 1519433859

DEDICATION

I don't know if it's possible to dedicate a book to a truck.
But that's what I'm doing. I once owned a green Chevy
truck. It is within that truck I learned how arrive on time
for work, take long-distance trips, open the passenger
door for ladies, and how to cry when nobody's watching.
It's where I grew up. I owned it for almost as long as I
can remember. Then, regrettably, I sold it to buy a nicer
one.

I've hated every truck I've had since.

ACKNOWLEDGMENTS

To all the people who read my writings every morning on Facebook, or my blog, thank you. It is because of your support and love that I'm even taking the time to compile these stories into book format. I'll be honest, words fail me. So I'll just say, thanks. And thank you once again.

SAIL IN A HANDBASKET

My wife, Jamie, went sailing with me yesterday. I tried to impress her by demonstrating how to sip beer while traveling at twelve knots.

She wasn't impressed.

The very first time I went sailing was to impress a girl, in 2001. I'll call her Millie, but that wasn't her real name. Millie's brother was the first-mate on a big cruising yacht in need of crew. At Millie's urging, I joined the ranks. But I wasn't a real sailor. Just some idiot in khaki shorts.

I looked like a math major.

There were four crew members aboard the seventy-foot cutter. We did whatever Millie's brother commanded. Sad to say, he turned out to be a real piece of work. He didn't like me one bit.

One weekend, two wealthy couples boarded for a three-day cruise in the Gulf. And these particular passengers were heavy tippers. For instance: one woman tipped me a fifty just for changing her pillowcases. I nearly fainted. For fifty bucks, I would've cleaned the hair out of her bathtub drain.

Barehanded.

Late one night, rumor had it that Millie's brother stole a hundred-dollar tip intended for me. I confronted him about it. He just laughed. One thing led to another, and soon I found myself trying to remove his head. But he was older, and a much better fighter.Finally, he pushed me overboard. Then tossed the hundred-dollar-bill into the night air.

"You want your money?" he yelled. "Swim for it."

Oh, I swam alright. For twenty minutes.

As it turned out, it was only a five-dollar tip.

TURKEY IN THE STRAW

They shot him in his right armpit. In Le Havre, France. They awarded him the Purple Heart for it. No one knows how he got wounded under his arm. And he wouldn't explain it either.

The Army whisked him away to a hospital in Italy, and left him to heal. There, he spent his days practicing mandolin. He was fire on that instrument, and picky about what he played. He would pretend to be offended if you asked him to play Kentucky tunes. "I only play real music," he'd say. "Not that hillbilly garbage."

Then he'd wink at you and play Turkey in the Straw.

Just because he could.

When he wasn't playing music, he carved. And God, could he carve. I have several of his wood figurines. He used an ugly pocket knife with a beat up brass handle, one he bought when he was twelve.

Every evening of his life, he polished the engine of his Steudabaker. That's what men did back then. It wasn't enough to keep the oil changed, and the engine running smooth.

It had to be clean, dammit.

That being said, he wasn't a car-man. He was a history buff. His greatest interest was the old West. Not just the West; Native Americans. Their culture, their artifacts, and ideas. Whenever you conversed with Grandaddy, you'd hear at least a few Native American proverbs. He was full of those. In fact, you waited for them.

But most of the time he'd fall asleep before he got to them.

With one hand resting in his right armpit.

FEMININE SIDE

Doctors aren't perfect. Last week, my doctor prescribed me a women's fertility medication by accident, instead of an antibiotic. No joke. But it wasn't his fault. His office accidentally called in the wrong prescription.

The first day on the meds: I noticed I had a stronger sense of smell.

Second day: I was a little grumpy, and my pants didn't fit.

Day three: the medication kicked in with full feminine-power. I woke up hungry, and my nipples hurt.

Jamie asked, "Do you want some eggs for breakfast?"

I misheard her. I thought she called me a "miserable fat-ass."

The next day, things went from bad to worse. I had cramps like I was about to give birth to a litter of goldfish. I also laughed for no reason, then cried. Then laughed again.

After which, I cried.

So, I drove to Krispy Kreme. I plowed through a dozen glazed donuts with both hands. Then, I returned

SEAN DIETRICH

home to watch Steel Magnolias on television. Afterward, I cried in the shower until we ran out of hot water.

Before bedtime, I cranked our thermostat down to forty degrees and redecorated the living room. Twice. That was the final straw, Jamie insisted I go to the doctor.

"What seems to be the problem?" the doc asked.

I sighed. "Things aren't good."

"Oh? Why don't you tell me what's wrong."

It took me a few minutes to stop sobbing.

"It's my wife," I said. "She doesn't pay attention to me. And I feel fat."

So, he wrote me a new script.

For a pap smear.

TUXES

The day of my wedding I woke up hungry. Deathly hungry. By lunchtime, it was life threatening. I got a bacon cheeseburger, two orders of fries, and a milkshake to-go. Then, I parked on the beach and wolfed it down.

I noticed my hands were shaking.

I glanced at the tuxedo hanging in the backseat of my truck. The suit was one size too small. I didn't know a thing about tuxes. I wished my father had been alive, maybe he would've known about them. He might've picked out a decent one. Or taught me how to put the damn thing on.

Who was I to decide on wardrobe? I would've rather had somebody assign me a costume. Like in our grade-school pageants. Back then, Miss Pam gave me the same stinky costume year after year. I was always the one in the tunic.

Holding a shepherd's crook.

That evening, I arrived at the wedding chapel after sunset. I was greeted by Jamie's daddy, and my uncle. They stood on the front stoop, eyeing their watches. They looked more awkward in their suits than I did.

"What'n the hell?" Jamie's daddy squinted at me. "You got your vest all catty-wampus."

"Sir?"

"Get over here," he said. "Don't you know how to dress?"

I guess not.

The two of them stripped me down right there in the parking lot.

"Hold still," Jamie's daddy said. "We're going to make you look pretty, son."

I know it was only figure of speech.

But it'd been a long time since anyone called me son.

ATTENTION

More than anything, my dog Ellie Mae wants my attention. She lives for it. If she's not getting it, she'll reorganize our waste basket with her teeth.

These days, everyone wants more attention. Not just dogs. Apparently, it's a researched thing. One researcher calls it, "...the phenomenon of narcissistic-social-media infatuation."

I found that quote on Twitter.

Before social media, we did without so much attention. No computers, no cellphones. We had rotary phones and Polaroid cameras. Our photo albums sat in the attic. No one ever saw our pictures. It's a good thing too, because I looked like a fat goat in our photos.

Before Facebook, I had about ten close friends. Well, make that nine. I unfriended Skid Reynolds the day I saw him drop his pants down around his ankles just to use a urinal.

He wasn't right.

Back then, when we wanted attention we entered the local talent show. Forget American Idol, we had the

Methodist Review. My first year competing, I lost to Charlotte Clark, who played Old Rugged Cross on a Coke bottle with a spatula.

Another hotbed for attention was the DeSoto Explorer, our local newspaper. I submitted several stories hoping for my big break. The editor – also my Sunday school teacher – told me I should consider applying for a job at the fertilizer plant.

But those are the things we did before attention was only a mouse-click away. You had to chase the spotlight. Beg for it, like a dog. Even knock down the garbage can, and roll around in trash if need be.

Like Ellie does.

DANGEROUS

Yesterday, I found a book at the flea-market, *The Pocket Dangerous Book for Boys.* I had to buy it, because Danger is my maiden name.

The truth is, I have a few things I'd like to add to the book.

For example: when a boy's wife asks how she looks in a pair of purple skinny-jeans. Welcome to dangerous territory my friend. Look, even if you hate purple, think twice. The only acceptable remark here is, "You look good enough to eat, darling." Anything less will get you ten stitches in a vulnerable region of your body.

And I mean vulnerable.

Another deadly situation: when a boy notices his wife behaving just like her mother. Danger. I repeat, danger. Do not under any circumstances draw comparisons between your wife and her mother. In fact, don't ever mention your mother-in-law. Never. Unless it's to say, "Hey honey, can I lift anything heavy for your mother? How about that chest of drawers again, maybe her concrete birdbath?"

Crisis averted.

Finally, let me tell you a story about a friend, boys. He was shopping with his wife. A certain female strutted past his line of vision. His wife noticed. She executed a classic AIAPAH maneuver. Pronounced, "eye-a-paw." Otherwise known as the Am-I-As-Pretty-As-Her question.

This is the most dangerous scenario known to boy.

I might as well tell you upfront, there's no correct answer to the AIAPAH question. None. The first word you speak, will be the first word of your eulogy.

My buddy found out the hard way.

His last words were, "Huh?"

FISHING WITH JOHN DEERE

I could hear her sputtering down the road. It sounded like she was riding a residential lawnmower. I squinted into the distance.

That's exactly what she was riding.

She wore a bikini top and had a cigarette balanced between her lips. Three fishing rods dangled from the back of the dilapidated John Deere. She rolled up slow, then parked beside the boat launch. The kayakers all gave her funny looks.

She paid them no mind.

The girl watched me hoist the mainsail of my boat. She was young, with rough leathery skin. Covered in tattoos. Much too worn out to be pretty; too pretty to be so worn out. In the short time it took me to rig my boat, she must've burned through eight cigarettes.

"Nice wheels." I nodded toward her lawnmower.

"Oh, that?" She laughed. "It belongs to the rehab. They let me drive it down here to go fishing."

I never learned her name, but she's been living at that women's rehab for six months. Before that, Walton

County Correctional Institution. Which is prison. Three years. "Prison ain't so bad," she explained. "The only bad part is the hard-ass work."

Sounds marvelous.

"Yeah," she said. "You learn a lot about yourself in prison. You think a lot."

She lit another cigarette. "Hell, I'm a country girl from Freeport. All I could think about in prison was going fishing. It reminds me of my daddy."

"Is your daddy a fisherman?"

"Was," she said. "He died while I was inside." She flashed a fake smile.

It wasn't any of my business.

But I'm glad she's got that lawnmower.

STUCK

Yesterday, was one of the hottest days ever recorded. It was a perfect day to get stuck in the bay with a dog.

A dog who lacks basic patience.

Let me back up. I've been stuck in the Choctawhatchee Bay a lot. So many times, it doesn't even surprise Jamie anymore.

Or me.

The first time I ever got stuck was on a fishing boat with two other fellas. They happened to be members of a cult. No joke. We had nothing to drink on the boat but a jug of Kool-Aid. When they passed the thermos to me, I decided to take my chances with dehydration.

Another instance was in a rowboat. I found myself stuck on an island. A real island. That day, a series of terrible events led to the perfect mess. My oarlocks broke, the current swept me into a grass-flat. I stayed stranded for seven hours.

I wrote my last will and testament on the back of a T-shirt.

Yesterday, however, was not nearly as fun-filled as

those previous times. Ellie and I sailed along when the wind died into a faint whisper. The sailboat ran up onto a sandbar. And just like that, we were stuck in the Choctawhatchee Bay on the hottest day in recorded Floridian history.

I went to fire up the motor. It sputtered and coughed. I tried again, its eyes rolled back into its carburetor. It finally went home to be with the Lord.

My phone battery was at four percent.

Home was two point nine miles away.

And Ellie was doing the pee-pee-dance.

WHO YOU CALLING SHRIMP?

I liked shrimp eight months before I was born. I'm serious. My mother claims she craved two things while pregnant with me: zucchini and shrimp. The cravings didn't go away after I was born. Those are still her favorite foods. And they're my favorite foods too.

We're a lot alike, me and Mother

Growing up, shrimp were hard to come by. Sure, you could buy them frozen in the supermarket, but those things aren't shrimp. Those are made in China. Probably in a lab. No sir, fresh-caught shrimp with the heads on are a different thing altogether.

When we first moved to Florida, neither Mother nor I had tasted fresh-caught shrimp. Not until a friend invited me to his family's pier for a low-country boil. His daddy dumped a boatload of seafood on a newspaper-covered table and told us to go to town.

My friend popped the head off a shrimp and sucked the brains out.

"See?" He demonstrated. "Eat it like this."

I made a face.

He grinned. "The head's where all the flavor is."

I pinched off a head and sucked. He was right. The heads were delicious. Soon, I'd mowed through so many shrimp my feet swelled up and my ears rang.

When we finished, my friend's daddy gave me a handful of Ziploc bags.

"Take plenty home for yourself," he told me.

So I loaded the baggies to full capacity.

My friend's daddy winked at me. "You must be stocking up for breakfast tomorrow, son."

"No sir." I shook my head. "These're for my mother."

SIMPLE AS BISCUITS

My wife, Jamie, makes biscuits whenever we're on vacation. It's a tradition. She makes them by hand. But they're a lot more than biscuits.

See, when we first married, Jamie was fresh out of culinary school. A bonafide chef. Her culinary interest had even taken her overseas. Part of her New Orleans education included time in Southern France, studying cuisine.

Then she met me. The furthest I'd ever traveled was Texarkana.

Jamie tried to educate me about cuisine, but it didn't take. She'd explain things like the biology of a perfect blanquette de veau. My eyes would usually glaze over.

Once, I responded by asking her about biscuits.

"Biscuits?" she said.

"Sure, can you make biscuits?"

She grew silent.

The truth was, I didn't know anything about food. I still drank Budweiser and ate sausages from a can. The only thing I knew about biscuits was the popping noise the Pilsbury tube made when you opened it.

I was only kidding with her, but it was too late. Jamie had made up her mind. She would master the American biscuit.

It took three years of experimentation. She practiced every morning with small batches. I ate so many biscuits I gained eleven pounds and doctors thought I had a thyroid problem.

Today, few people know about Jamie's biscuits. She doesn't talk about them. She doesn't like the limelight. And besides, she only cooks them on vacation.

But it still impresses me, that while some ambitious chefs are working on their resumes, others like Jamie have chosen another route.

And just work on their biscuits.

MARY OF BREWTON

I took my wife's mother fishing yesterday. Just outside Panacea, Florida. We had a marvelous time. We even wore matching shirts and drank matching iced teas. With matching sprigs of mint. While we fished, Miss Mary took the opportunity to tell me a few stories.

"When I was a girl," Mary explained. "The high school in Brewton would host a boy's basketball tournament. It was wonderful. Every year, boys came from all over. They practically filled up our town. Each direction you looked: boys, boys, and more boys."

She paused.

"Mary?" I asked. "Everything okay?"

"Yes, fine. What was I saying again?"

"Basketball."

"Oh yes, that's right. So many good-looking boys."

"You already said that part."

"Well," she went on. "Mother and Daddy would let the basketball players stay at our house. They slept upstairs." Mary flashed a little grin. "For a teenage girl like me, it was Christmas. I'd come down to breakfast every morning and see six boys at the table, waiting for me. All my girlfriends were jealous."

She let out a sigh. "Oh my, we'd play badminton in the backyard. Girls against boys. Heavens, those young men were such fine athletes. So strong. Such broad shoulders."

"Alright," I interrupted. "Can we do a different story?"

She closed her eyes and leaned back into her chair. "Back then, basketball shorts weren't as big and baggy as they are today."

"Miss Mary, what do you say we listen to the radio?"

"Those basketball shorts were so short."

"Okay, I really think..."

"And so very tight-fitting."

HIKING WITH YOU

"Look!" shrieked Jamie. "A white spider."

The spider on the ground was huge. It looked like a white football with legs. Jamie knows I hate spiders more than anything. Especially white ones.

"Are we lost?" asked Jamie.

I laughed at her question. Of course, we weren't lost. We were on the Ochlockonee Bay Trail. I had no earthly idea where on the trail we were. But I knew we were on it.

If you've never hiked the Ochlockonee Bay Trail, you don't know what you're missing. It's a grassy kind of hell, covered in spiders, water moccasins, and other things that'll loosen your bowels right up.

"I'm thirsty," Jamie whined.

I don't know how she could've been. Jamie had drained all three bottles of our water and plowed through all four granola bars.

Four.

I scanned the horizon. All landmarks looked the same, nothing but trees and grass. I wasn't sure we'd ever see home again. I closed my eyes and did some quick calculating. If my math was correct, it would take approximately two hours for a black bear to rip our intestines through our nostrils, then pick his teeth with our collar bones.

And after wandering five hours in one-hundred-eight-degree weather, all I wanted to do was eat a granola bar. No such luck. Thanks to Jamie, all we had left was a backpack full of jack-squat.

"Oh my God, look!" Jamie leapt up and shouted.

"What is it?" I said. "You see our car?"

"No, a white spider just ran across the back of your neck."

WHAT I LIKE ABOUT LISTS

As a husband, there's nothing that tests my marital grit like grocery lists. It's true. In thirteen years, I've yet to make a successful trip. I forget things, or worse, buy the wrong brand of toilet paper.

Still, I don't mind zipping off to the store. I find the aisles of the supermarket to be tranquilizing. Especially the Campbell's soup aisle. The only request I make before going is that I be provided with an accurate list. One with details. Otherwise, I'm liable to return home with a puppy and a bag of Fritos.

Here's an example: Jamie wrote me out a list yesterday. The list read, "pepper, fish, tampons." That was all. She might as well have given me a copy of the Wall Street Journal and a can of Bud Light.

I needed specifics.

What did she mean by pepper? Did she want a red bell pepper, or a can of black pepper? What about the fish? Did she want frozen cod, imported snapper, or a can of sardines?

And that brings us to tampons.

There must be sixty-seven different kinds of tampons. They come in varieties like: light, sport, regular, pearl, super, super-super, super-duper, and straight-jacket.

The cashier gave me a little grin when I checked out.

"You're a good man for buying these," she said. "But can I give you a little friendly advice?"

"Yes ma'am."

"We have a special on chocolate bars, aisle six." She winked.

"Thanks, but no thanks," I said. "Chocolate wouldn't go well with the sardines she put on my list."

SHELLS

The first time I saw a seashell was in third grade. Someone in class brought it for show and tell.

The teacher passed it around the room. We all took turns holding it up to our rural ears, listening to the Gulf of Mexico. And it worked. You could hear the whispering sound of waves. Then, everyone in class got a tiny seashell as a souvenir. But you couldn't hear the Gulf in those little things.

God knows, I listened for it.

The Gulf of Mexico seemed like a planet of its own. My grandfather was the only person in my family who had even seen it, long ago. He told me it was magnificent.

And I took his word for it, since I only had my little seashell to go by.

Two summers after Daddy died, I finally saw the Gulf. Our cabin was right on the beach. Though I couldn't tell you what the cabin's inside looked like, I didn't spend much time indoors. I was too busy staring at the green water, searching for more seashells.

Mostly, I didn't leave my beach chair. All week. I sat right up near the water. It wasn't that I was enjoying myself, I was more hypnotized than anything.

Three nights in a row, I fell asleep in my beach chair. Mother let me sleep out there until the wee hours of the morning. And she must've come out at some point to cover me up, because whenever I awoke there would be a strange blanket draped over me.

And a few new seashells down at my feet.

SAILING WITH ME

"I'll never go sailing with you again," she said.

Jamie was overreacting. Our predicament wasn't my fault. I can't help it that Indian Pass is crawling with bullsharks. Likewise, I can't help it that bullsharks like to swim next to small sailboats. Neither can I help it that my small racing craft is only big enough for one person.

All I know is, Jamie wanted to go sailing. So that morning, I strapped her to the bow of the boat, and by George, we went sailing.

The first bullshark we saw was a beauty. I believe it was a teenage shark because its fin was the size of my hand. The next creature we saw must've been the first one's older brother. It was a monstrosity, with a dorsal fin the size of a refrigerator.

Jamie screamed.

"Hey," I said. "Don't move. You'll tip the boat if you move like that."

But she paid me no mind. She tried to crawl back to the cockpit, and that was it. *The S.S. Squirrel* went belly up. We plunged into the shark infested water, beer coozies and all. The last thing I remember was Jamie's hindquarters pressed up against my face.

"You dumbass!" she said, bobbing in the water.

"Me?" I said. " What'd I do? You're the one who tipped the boat."

"Sean, you know what happens when you tell me not to do something."

My smile faded, and my face became serious.

"What?" she yelled. "You see a shark?"

"Jamie," I said. "Whatever you do, please don't let me watch baseball tonight."

BAD DOGS

She sleeps beside my bed. That's her spot, every single night.

I'm not sure how we became such good friends. After all, we don't have much in common, not really. We don't speak the same language, we don't eat the same things. And she never cleans up after herself.

Never.

Furthermore, her breath stinks, and she chews with her mouth open. She's selfish, she's greedy, impulsive, lazy, wasteful, and she always has to be the center of attention.

One more thing, and it embarrasses me to say it: she steals.

She has no sense of guilt, like I do. None. When she lays her head down to sleep, she feels no remorse for her sins. She doesn't even know what sins are.

If she did, she'd probably try to eat them.

I wish you knew her, then you'd know what I'm talking about. You'd see how demanding she is. Then, you'd ask me how I put up with such a spoiled creature.

Or why.

And I wouldn't be able to come up with a good answer.

Because the truth is, sometimes I get this feeling. And I get it a lot, when I watch her sleep. I think about the ten dogs I've had in my life. About how they've gone on to the other side without me, one by one. I remember their open-mouthed smiles, and their favorite toys. I still have their collars. I wish they were all right here with me. Right now. I'd like to feel their love just one more time.

When I see her sleeping beside my bed, I do.

SEW RIGHT

She's sewed for practically all her life.

When she was twelve, she'd go downtown and stare into the shop windows at Weaver's. She'd sketch a few fashion designs on a notepad, then dart back home to replicate them.

When I was a boy, she made my clothes. Nearly everything I wore. Mine were the only shirts in the school without tags. "Why don't my shirts have tags?" I'd ask.

"Because," she'd answer. "Fancy clothes don't need tags."

Fancy or not, I wanted tags like the other kids. Everyone had labels inside their collars. How else would I know if my shirt was right-side-out?

So my mother sent off for mail-order printed tags. She sewed them into every article of my wardrobe. Even my ball caps.

"Property of Sean Dietrich," the tag read. Then it listed my home address, just in case someone ever needed to air-mail me a lost pair of my underpants.

Like most boys, I was rough on my clothes. A tall basket sat next to my mother's sewing machine where I deposited ripped jeans and tattered shirts for mending. And that woman must've spent half her life patching up my grass-stained clothes.

And on the day I left home, she met me at the door with a little tin box. One of her sewing kits. It was filled with needles, buttons, thread, and thimbles.

"What's this for?" I asked.

"For you," she said. "It might come in handy, you know, when I'm not around."

Well then, I don't want it.

Not ever.

NECKTIES

"Lord," Jamie's mother said. "Sometimes, I didn't want anyone to know that Jamie was my child."

When I asked Miss Mary why she would say such a thing, she was all too happy to tell me.

"Well," Mary explained. "As a young girl, Jamie wore men's clothing. She refused to wear anything else. Button down shirts, wide brimmed hats, and even neckties. It nearly drove me to the bottle." Miss Mary laughed. "I took Jamie shopping, to buy some new clothes, so she'd at least look decent in public. I told her I'd buy her anything she liked. Anything. Just so she'd quit wearing neckties."

Mary buried her face in her hands and sighed. "Jamie was making me into the laughing stock of Brewton with those neckties."

I nodded, even though I'm pretty sure the last part was an exaggeration.

"But you see," said Miss Mary. "It's hard to shop with Jamie, she's an indecisive shopper."

Thirteen years of marriage. You're preaching to the

choir, sister.

"Jamie would keep us at the store all day. She'd try on every stitch of clothing in the place, and still not find an outfit she liked.

"So, I'd take her to another store. That child didn't want anything but a new necktie, and some Milk Duds." Miss Mary scoffed. "I thought about leaving her there for good."

"So what'd you do?" I asked.

"I gave up trying and let her have all of Boyd's and Jim's old clothes." Miss Mary smiled. "Back when I was a girl, I wish I'd been bold enough to be myself, like Jamie."

Don't we all Miss Mary.

Don't we all.

THINGS I LOVE

Longwinded Facebook rants. People love to complain on Facebook for everyone to see. Then, other folks come along and complain about all the complaining on Facebook. And now, I'm complaining about the people who complain about all the complaining. And round and round it goes.

Well.

I've decided to add a rant of my own to the pile.

THINGS I LOVE
By Sean "Never-Was" Dietrich

The first thing I love about Facebook is photos. Old ones. They touch me. Photographs of people, both alive and deceased. The older the better. In people's photos, I see how other folks live, and their families. Then, I realize other folks' aunts are just as off-kilter as mine. Especially if their aunts start drinking gin before noon.

And then I feel less alone.

Another thing I love: kids losing their teeth, learning to ride bikes, or eating popsicles. The truth is, Jamie and I weren't lucky enough to have children. We missed out on the blessings of parenthood. But each morning on Facebook, when I watch someone's baby smile at the camera, I feel a little tickle in my stomach. And I love that.

Dogs. I believe I must've been one in a past life. Or, maybe I just like naps and foul-smelling things. Facebook is seventy percent dogs. These canine pictures and videos are the reason I get out of bed. And don't forget animal adoptions. Last year alone, Facebook prompted nearly eight million animal rescues.

Eight-cotton-picking million.

But what I love about Facebook most, is people. People getting a piece of the spotlight. See, in the old days you were either famous, or you weren't. If you were popular, you got attention. If you weren't, they'd tie an apron around you and make you cook meatloaf for your husband and twelve kids. And that was life.

Not anymore. On Facebook, you're as important as any celebrity. Your pictures matter. Your videos, your stories, your favorite songs, even your rants. They somehow matter. All of them.

At least they do to me.

RASCAL

Rascal Lovebug Sassy Martin-Dietrich turned twenty this August. Her joints hurt, she has a thyroid problem, she gets confused from time to time, she urinates on my clothes, and she's virtually deaf.

Otherwise, she's in pretty good shape for a twenty-year-old.

My wife, Jamie, found Rascal two decades ago, in the middle of the night. It happened when Jamie spotted a kitten-shaped blur darting across the highway. Jamie swerved and nearly wrecked trying to dodge the little creature.

Right off the bat, Rascal became like Jamie's child. And feline motherhood presented some unseen challenges. For one: Rascal didn't care for a newspaper-bathroom system. Instead, she preferred to do her business on the kitchen counter. Second: as it turns out, cats can't survive on a diet of Campbell's Chicken Noodle Soup and Doritos.

They're not like me.

When I met Rascal, she was already a seven-year-old

package of piss and vinegar. She didn't warm up to me at first. But that all changed when she vomited on my pillow. After that incident, something shifted in our relationship and she trusted me. She proved it by leaving me little gifts.

Often.

But I can't complain, because everything Rascal does is endearing. For instance: she has a special way of screaming when she's hungry – at four in the morning. She makes the same sound your grandmother might make if she's fallen and broken her hip. Jamie and I take turns waking up in the middle of the night to replenish Rascal's food bowl. I stroke Rascal's soft fur while she eats.

And ask God to let her live until she's sixty.

CHRISTOPHER

Christopher and I were cowboys. It was more than play. We believed we were cattle rustlers. Most days, we left the house dressed like child-sized versions of the Malboro Man.

The Magnificent Two. That's what we called ourselves. Initially, Christopher wanted to use the names Lone Ranger and Tonto. But I didn't like that idea one bit. I'd rather eat dirt and bark at the moon than be anyone's Tonto.

Television westerns were what we lived for. Gunsmoke, Bonanza, and Big Valley were the blueprints for our playtime.

We were expert marksman with our dummy Winchester rifles and peacemakers. I must've killed more bandits and bloodthirsty savages than John Wayne and all the Cartwrights combined.

Those cap guns of ours never missed.

The two of us even wore our cowboy hats to kindergarten. But the teacher wouldn't allow us to wear them in class. Teacher also made us check our iron at the front door. Still, it made no difference.

Christopher always carried a single-shooter on his ankle.

Once, Christopher was out of school for two whole weeks. I asked my mother why he was absent. She sat me down and explained Christopher had bad kidneys. His parents had taken him to Colorado to let the doctors try to fix him.

She said he wouldn't be back for a while.

We packaged up two brand new cap guns, a ten-gallon hat, and a few packs of candy cigarettes. We mailed them off to Colorado.

I understand they buried Christopher with those cap guns.

A FINE GOOSENECK

Last fall, we drove to Goose Creek, South Carolina to visit my elderly aunt for her birthday. I didn't want to go, but Jamie insisted it was the right thing to do.

We left town at ten o'clock in the evening to avoid traffic. I brought along an extra large thermos of coffee to help me stay alert through the night. And, I did more than stay alert. After tossing back three cups, I was singing back-up for Willie Nelson, playing drum solos on the steering wheel.

By the time we reached Yulee, Georgia I'd consumed six cups total, and had pulled over to pee seventy times. Jamie slept in the seat beside me, her mouth gaped open. To entertain myself, I placed a penny in her open mouth. One, then another. When I got to twelve cents, she woke up.

And that's how I lost my right molar.

Seven in the morning: we rolled through Savannah, Georgia. I looked into the visor mirror. My eyes were bloodshot, I'd lost almost five pounds, and I had to pee like Seabiscuit.

I should've pulled over, but I didn't. We were making good time.

When we arrived in Goose Creek, I was up to eleven cups of coffee altogether. I was a human water-balloon. I bounced my knees up and down, but it did no good. I was about to start leaking.

When we finally pulled into my aunt's driveway, she and my cousins tore off the front porch to take turns squeezing me. And oh, how they squeezed.

Until they were sorry.

CHUBBY

I was a chubby child. But I wasn't always that way. When I was eight, I was as lean as goat leg. Nothing but skin, muscle, and a little bit of gas from time to time. Mother said I was so skinny, I had to stand up twice just to make a shadow.

But everything changed when I hit eleven. Overnight, I shot up eight whole inches. And I grew rounder too. My pants got tight, my cheeks became rosy, and my appetite was out of control.

I ate twice the amount my classmates did. I couldn't help it, I was always famished. Instead of one sandwich for lunch, Mother had to pack me two. Sometimes three.

Along with a baggie of Doritos.

And Twinkies.

Finally, my mother took me to the doctor to see if something was wrong with me.

"No, there's nothing wrong with him," the physician said. "He's a growing boy. I was the same way when I was his age." He patted my belly. "A little butterball. He just needs to eat healthier."

Butterball?

When my mother pressed the doctor for advice, he suggested I give up mashed potatoes, swear off barbecue, and read my Bible. I'm almost certain my mother paid him to say the last part.

When I asked the doctor if I could still eat Twinkies, he just chuckled and said, "Maybe after you're married, son." Then, he wrote me a prescription for spinach salads and rice cakes. To finish up our consult, the doctor asked me which flavor of sucker I wanted.

Easy.

Butterscotch, strawberry, watermelon, green apple, lemon, and cherry.

AUNT MILENA

My mother had a blind aunt named Milena. She's passed now. God rest her soul. Milena lived by herself, and could do almost anything on her own. She made coffee, paid bills, baked brownies, and even did her own shopping.

She had a guide dog named Whistler. But he and I weren't friendly. He didn't like to play.

He was all business.

Aunt Milena was old when I knew her. She carried a long folding cane when she and Whistler went to the grocery store. She'd grab one of the young supermarket employees to guide her around the aisles. Before she'd leave the store, she'd say something like, "Thanks for the help. Come by and visit me sometime."

I never knew anyone to take her up on the offer.

Too bad, because Milena was a skilled conversationalist. Conversation was Milena's favorite form of entertainment.

Once, I asked Aunt Milena what she dreamed about.

"Dream?" she said. "Oh, I dream about the same

things you do, I suppose. About meeting people, touching things, smelling things."

"What about seeing?" I asked. "Can you see in your dreams?"

She thought for a moment. "Well, I don't really know. I've never seen before. My dreams appear to me the same as my life does."

"Well, what's that look like?"

"Oh, it's lovely." She tilted her head up toward the ceiling. "It looks like everything, pressed all together. Both dark and light. Tall and short, small and big, all at the same time."

"Huh?"

"It looks like the water and sky," she said. "On a cloudless day."

"But, how do you know what that looks like?"

"I don't." She smiled. "I'm just guessing."

LIONEL

Lionel was my childhood friend. Lionel was different. He had a white mother and a black father. To the black children, Lionel was white. To the white kids, Lionel was black.

As a result, Lionel didn't fit in.

Lionel once told me he wasn't sure what he really was. Black or white. It seemed like an easy problem to my ten-year-old imagination. I suggested Lionel forget colors, and consider himself a lion. Lion, for Lionel. He loved the idea. When I asked him to pick an animal for me, he chose a billy goat.

"But don't lions eat goats?" I asked.

"Nope," he assured me. "Not this lion."

So, that's what we became. Lion and billy goat. He fit his part well. He was athletic and fast. I wasn't sure I fit my part as well as he did, because I didn't eat tin cans or poop standing up.

At least not much.

Once, a few older boys began making fun of Lionel. I won't repeat the things they said, because I don't think anyone should have to hear them. Not ever. After a few minutes of their insults, one of the older boys took to throwing bits of gravel at Lionel. A rock hit him on the lip.

That did it.

My face got hot and I charged that bully with everything I had in me. Shoulder first. We hit the ground rolling. I'm glad my mother wasn't around, because I used language that would've landed me in the electric chair – for life.

When it was all over, I got in bad trouble for ramming that bully. But I wasn't sorry, because Lionel was my friend.

And by God, that's what billy goats do.

CONFIDENCE

"Get out of this car," Mother said. "Show that football coach what you're made of."

"I'm scared," I said.

"You've got to have faith in yourself. Believe you can do it."

I sighed. "But what if I fail?"

"Then I'll disown you and move to Vegas."

"Huh?"

"I'm only kidding." She patted my leg. "Look, I know God didn't give you confidence. But don't doubt yourself, get out there and try."

She was right. I wasn't born with the confidence my friends had. Once, the baseball coach asked me if I wanted to play first base. I answered, "Sure, I'd love to. If you don't mind losing every game."

They made me an understudy for the batboy.

When I was older, they asked me to play the lead role in the school musical. I didn't sleep for two nights and lost six pounds. I told the director I'd be more comfortable handing out programs wearing a ski mask.

He shook his head at me. "We already have someone for programs," he said. "You can be the understudy for the batboy again."

Coach was also our director.

Despite my timidness, my mother somehow believed in me. For many years, she was the only one who did. And on that particular day, she believed I could be a defensive tackle.

The football tryouts lasted half the day. When I walked back to the car, Mother asked how things went.

"Things went great!" I told her.

"See?" She smiled. "That's what happens when you believe in yourself. What position are you?"

Understudy for the batboy.

COMPANY

"Out of town company," Daddy said. "That's the real test of a man. If you want to see what a man's made of, wait until he has company visiting."

"Company?" I asked.

"Yep," he explained. "When a man has houseguests, his manners are put to the test."

Daddy turned out to be right. Just last month, we had my cousins stay with us. My cousins are from Godless New Jersey. Both of them talk funny. They say things like "you guys," "what's up," and "soda pop."

They also use a particular swear word – beginning with the sixth letter of the alphabet – that I won't repeat in this story.

Because my mother reads these things.

Jamie and I fixed up the guest bedroom and stocked the pantry. Jamie even made an arrangement from fresh cut magnolias for the den. We tried to make our guests comfortable, we even planned suppers around them.

One night for supper, we put out a real spread. We made collards, cheese grits, and pulled pork sandwiches.

"What is that horrible smell?" my cousin asked. "It smells like a rotten cat in here."

"The smell?" I said. "It's only collards."

My hospitality was being put to the test.

"What about that? What's all that yellow crap?" He pointed to the pot on the stove.

"This *crap*?" I said. "These're grits."

"Ugh, gross." He wrinkled his face.

I closed my eyes and recited the Lord's Prayer silently.

Then the Pledge of Allegiance.

"What about that pot?" He nodded toward the barbecued pork.

"What's all that $#!+ right there?"

"Oh this?" I said. "This is my famous raccoon liver stew."

He covered his mouth.

"Don't worry," I told him. "I saved the tail for you."

FOUR HOURS SOUTH OF FAYETTEVILLE

If you ride I-95 south from Fayetteville you'll eventually hit Savannah. And, if you make the drive at night, it's easy. The highway is almost empty. You can travel ninety-one miles per hour if you want.

That's exactly what my mother did.

After my father died, Mother was a raw nerve. If anyone looked at her wrong, she'd either cuss or break down in tears. You never knew which to expect. As a result, things between her and my aunt grew tense.

One night in Fayetteville, my aunt and my mother erupted into an all-out brawl. It wasn't pretty. In truth, it was bound to happen. They'd been fussing all week. But I knew it wasn't all my aunt's fault.

The truth was, my mother just needed someone to yell at.

Mother squealed out of my aunt's driveway and shot her arm out the window. She used a finger I didn't even know she had. And we were gone.

We drove until we hit a dilapidated motel in

Savannah.

"We're not going home," Mother said. "Not yet. We're going to have fun, dammit." She wiped the running mascara from her eyes. "Fun!"

And that's what we did.

For two weeks, Savannah was our Disneyworld. We went on haunted tours, visited historic homes, and ate expensive food. And one day, we even took a road trip to Tybee Island. A thirty-minute drive east toward the Atlantic. When we crossed over the first bridge, Mother slammed on the brakes and pulled over.

She was silent.

We were all bone-silent.

And that was the first time we saw the ocean.

SWEET OR HALF-SWEET

Iced tea. I like mine sweet enough to break your jaw; Jamie likes hers half sweet.

When we first married, we drank a lot of iced tea. Morning, afternoon, and night. We drank it not because we lived in the South, but because we had no air conditioning in our ratty apartment.

None.

In only one summer, we destroyed every piece of furniture we owned with moisture rings from tea glasses. Life without a functioning AC was misery. We'd recline on the couch and press cold glasses against the sides of our necks. And of course, we'd complain about the heat.

We happen to be excellent complainers.

When we moved into a new place, we finally had a functioning air conditioner. You would've thought we won the lottery. We'd sit in front of the vent and let it blow in our faces. For the first time in our young marriage, we could relax in the den without leaving sweat stains on the sofa.

Over the years, we bought nicer furniture. A new

couch, a new coffee table, and we started using coasters. After all, that's what adults do. We quit sipping so much iced tea, we bought better insurance, and I even started cutting our grass regularly.

Well, semi-regularly.

But sometimes, on Sunday afternoons, or at barbecues, I'll fix Jamie and I both iced teas. We'll press the glasses against our foreheads like we used to. Then, we'll look at each other with half-smiles and talk about our pathetic first apartment. About how dank and miserable it was.

And how much we miss it.

NO BIG THING

I've always believed something big would happen to me. And the truth is, I haven't wanted to believe that. But the belief is one passed down from my mother. She told me to always keep my eyes open, to wait for that thing. "It's on its way," she'd say.

Well.

I'm sorry Mother, it's been thirty-three years and nothing's happened yet.

I'm not famous, I'm not rich, and I didn't win anything. In fact, I've never won anything. I've never even traveled outside the U.S – unless you count Tijuana. And the most notable thing I've ever done was stay awake for two days. But that was only because my truck broke down outside Possum Trot, Alabama.

Let's see. What else.

I didn't have many girlfriends. And the ones I did have thought I was boring. I know this because they told me so. You know what else is boring? I grew up on a boring farm where I milked goats.

That's right.

Goats.

More about me: I've never eaten a filet mignon, I hate scotch, and sometimes, I still sit down to pee like my mother taught me when I was a toddler.

Course of habit.

I've owned a handful of mutts, one car, seven trucks, and totaled three. Trucks, not dogs. I love liver and onions, and Spongebob Squarepants, too. My back is covered in unsightly hair, and I get gout sometimes. I talk with my mouth full, and I'm pretty sure I snore. Big things don't happen to people like me.

And I'm happy they don't.

Because I'd be miserable if they did.

.

SKIP

I'm going to call him Skip, but that's not his real name. I met him on the side of Highway 10, outside Tallahassee. He stood next to an old Dodge, watching traffic zoom by.

Skip's alternator had gone to be with Jesus.

I don't often pick up strangers, but it was too hot to let anyone stand next to a broke-down Dodge.

When I shook Skip's hand, I noticed he looked familiar. Two bushy gray eyebrows, a toothy smile, and a pair of long knobby legs. And that laugh. Skip had a wide-mouthed, animated laugh. Like Mister Ed.

My father laughed like Mister Ed.

Skip rode in the passenger seat beside me, chatting up a blue streak. I tried not to stare at him, but I couldn't help it. The fella beside me could've been my daddy's twin.

And while Skip talked, I thought about Daddy. I imagined what he'd look like if he were alive. The things we might talk about while riding in the truck. Daddy'd probably talk about baseball pitchers and batting averages. Maybe I'd talk about Jamie, or boats. Then, maybe we'd flip on the radio and let Hank Williams howl at us while we ate spicy pork rinds.

Maybe.

I dropped Skip off at Publix to wait for his wife. He shook my hand again and said, "Thanks buddy. You helped me out a lot, the sun would've burned me into a tater tot if you wouldn't have come along."

I let out a little snort.

Because I laugh a lot like Mister Ed, too.

SIX DAYS FOURTEEN HOURS
TWENTY-SEVEN MINUTES

Well hell, I finally did it. I ruined my phone. I was all the way in Midway, Georgia when it happened. I'm too embarrassed to tell you how. It wasn't pretty. The motel plumber was even more embarrassed than me. The first thing he did was tell his assistant to bring him a monkey wrench and a whiskey sour.

Subsequently, I've been without a phone six days, fourteen hours, and twenty-seven minutes. But the withdrawals started after only a few seconds. I experienced cold sweats, and I kept hearing a faint ringing coming from my pocket.

Like my mother was calling.

The next day, nothing seemed right. I felt stuck in the dark ages. To read emails, I visited the local library. Their PC was ancient. The librarian used a pull-cord to fire the thing up before logging me in. But it didn't work. The computer needed new spark plugs.

Then there's navigation. Without a phone-GPS, it's almost impossible. I pulled over for directions. The man working at the gas station was from Moscow. The only English he knew was, "My name is Vadim, which way for man bathrooms, please?"

I answered with the only bit of Russian I knew: Сделайте меня богатым.

The following morning, I awoke disoriented. I had no idea what time it was. I stumbled into the motel cafe, still half-asleep. I asked the waitress for a breakfast menu.

"Breakfast?" She gave me a funny look. "It's three in the afternoon, sweet cheeks."

"Just bring me anything," I said.

She brought me a monkey wrench and a whiskey sour.

MEAN PEOPLE

A a boy, I wish someone would've told me that some people just won't like you. No matter how nice you are. Some people just won't like the look of your face.

Take, for instance, Phil. He told the entire school bus I smelled like a filthy pig's hindparts. Everyone got a big chuckle out of that. I even caught the bus driver, laughing. She blamed it on Phil's talent for comedy.

To be fair, Phil did have a gift.

Ninth grade: Brittany, from math class hated me. She was three-times my size, and she only knew six words. One word was my name, the other five were swear words.

The teacher took me aside once. "Look honey," she said. "Don't take Brittany's abuse personal. I think she likes you."

Well, if my teacher's theory is correct, then old man Jacob must've idolized me. Jacob was fifty years my senior. We were a two-man sheetrock crew. The old buzzard treated me like a staircase.

Finally, one day I hit my breaking point.

"Jacob," I asked. "Why're you always so mean to me?"

"Because," he said. "I had a terrible childhood, my daddy called me stupid." He sighed. "I put you down to make myself feel better."

"Does it make you feel better?"

"Sure it does." He shrugged. "Try it yourself. Go on, insult me."

So I tried.

"Mister Jacob," I said. "I think you're the best sheetrocker in the business. And I've learned a lot from you. Furthermore, I think you're pretty smart."

He looked at me.

"Damn son," he said. "Now you're just being cruel."

MY GIRLS

My mother and sister didn't always get along. That's because both of them have fiery personalities. They're both strong willed. My sister has a hot temper, and she's stubborn.

And Mother wrote the book on such things.

I can remember arguments between them lasting late into the night. And even though their squabbles didn't involve me, I seemed to be around for most of them.

During one such argument, my mother got so worked up she threw a handful of flour at my sister. It looked like it was snowing in the kitchen. My sister went to the pantry and found a bag of grits. The two of them battled it out.

Handful by handful.

When I stepped in to break things up, someone threw a fistful of grits into my eyes by accident.

I yelped like a girl.

The two of them fell into a fit of laughter. They spent the next morning mopping the kitchen and cleaning counters while I was busy learning to read braille.

These days, my mother and sister get along fine. Oh sure, the two of them have ups and downs. Sometimes they fuss and go a few days without talking.

But not that often.

Sometimes, they'll stay up all night playing Scrabble. Mother will beat the pants of my sister. Mother always wins at Scrabble. And my sister is always hopping mad when she does. Then, they'll eat chocolate – they love chocolate. They'll talk about things and tell each other important secrets. Ones they'd never tell me.

Not in a million years.

Because some secrets are best kept between sisters.

THE RECYCLISTS

Recycle everything. Because if you don't, God will kill you. And if by chance God is busy, and can't kill you, He'll deputize your wife to do it.

She's probably already been sworn in.

However, if you're married, you probably already recycle. If you aren't sure whether you're married, try this: go into your laundry room for a peek. See it? An overflowing plastic tub of beer cans, Land's End catalogs, and ketchup bottles.

You, my friend, have a wife.

Look, I know recycling is good for the environment. But to be quite honest, it feels unnatural to save all that trash. It's an affront to the way I was raised.

I didn't grow up recycling. I'd never even heard the term until my buddy's daddy used it. We'd drink Coca-Cola all day until our kidneys pickled.

His daddy would make a joke. "We recycle Coke in this household, boys. It ain't cheap. Use the bathroom down the hall."

I never drank Coke at my buddy's again.

My mother, however, did recycle one thing. Hand-me-down clothes. Once per year, I inherited a garbage bag full of foul-smelling vestments from my older cousin Ernie. After a good washing, they still smelled bad. I'm convinced Ernie rode bareback in the goat rodeo wearing those blue jeans.

Eventually, when my inherited clothes were about to disintegrate from several decades of use, I passed them on to my sister. Boy's clothes. Sometimes, people at church would plug their noses and tell Mother how cute her two fetid-smelling boys looked.

Mother would smile and say, "Thanks, we recycle."

IT'S IN THE DRINKING WATER

I was raised going to church. It's part of who I am. Like many of my friends, I grew up in the heart of the Bible Belt. Religion was in our drinking water, you couldn't avoid it.

No more than you could avoid talking like a hick.

My daddy's parents were staunch German Catholics. Two of my great-aunts were nuns. Masses were in Latin. Daddy told me to answer anything I heard in church with, "Miserere mei Deus." Which means: Lord have mercy.

Occasionally, I still use the phrase.

But now I say it during baseball games.

My mother was Lutheran – hardcore. She's just like a lot of Lutherans. She believes in the healing power of lemon chicken casserole, macaroni and cheese, and pound cake. Baked in foil-covered dishes.

You can keep the dishes.

My friend Charles was raised atheist. He's like a brother to me, but I can't begin to understand what his childhood must've been like.

"My parents didn't have many friends," said Charles. "They were scientists. They questioned everything, trusted no one."

Sounds fun.

Charles explained, "I thought church-folks were just members of a big social club. Looking for an excuse to hang out with their friends. Singing, having potlucks, eating fried chicken and potato salad."

Don't forget biscuits, Charles.

He shook his head. "I grew up thinking y'all were nicey-nice, soft people. Folks who used the idea of God to help you through hard times. Because you were too weak to handle it on your own."

I couldn't have said it any better, Charles. Not even if I tried.

Lord, have mercy.

FRIED

Occasionally, I get a hankering for fried chicken. But I don't want just any chicken. I want Kentucky Fried Chicken. Original recipe. In a big, striped bucket.

I ought to be ashamed of myself for admitting such.

As a boy, we ate KFC every blessed Friday night. As far back as I can remember. When Daddy got home on Friday evenings, he'd honk the horn in the driveway. I'd march my chubby little legs outside and help him muscle the big bucket into the kitchen.

One summer, my uncle, Hoyt, got a part-time job working at Kentucky Fried Chicken. It was the greatest summer of my entire existence. The best part was they allowed Hoyt to give free chicken to his family. I was that family.

I gained eight pounds in six days.

At the time, KFC still hand-battered chicken. That's what made it taste so good. There's a big difference between the hand-battered and whatever the other kind is.

After spending three months on the Colonel's front

lines, damned if Hoyt didn't figure out KFC's famous recipe. A secret blend of eleven spices.

Passed down from Moses himself.

One Friday night, Hoyt cooked fried chicken for the entire family. All that frying turned our kitchen into a grease pit. The floors became so slick I could ice skate on them. And that's exactly what I did. While Hoyt tended the skillet, I spun circles on the floor like Peggy Fleming.

As it turned out, I never tasted Hoyt's fried chicken.

And the doctor said my tailbone would never be the same.

MARY

"Growing up in Brewton was marvelous," said my mother-in-law, Mary. "We had wonderful childhoods before technology came along."

Miss Mary talks like an Alabamian, drawing out her vowels. To me, Mary sounds like a Vivien Leigh recording played at half-speed.

"Our town was very rural," Miss Mary said. "And uppity at the same time. That's how small Alabama towns are."

I asked her to explain.

She was glad to.

"My family was an ordinary Brewton family. Mother and Daddy weren't poor, but they weren't rich. They lived in the middle of town. You would've thought I'd be a prim and proper in-town girl, but I wasn't. At least not all the way."

"How do you mean?" I asked.

"Well," Mary went on to say. "I had the strangest pets you ever heard of. I had a pet raccoon once. He washed his hands in his water bowl before supper every single night. Like this." Miss Mary demonstrated. "I also had a pet squirrel, a black snake, three geckos, stray cats, and a teenage possum."

I interrupted. "Teenage?"

"Yes, you know, a possum that's going through puberty."

How silly of me.

"I also had a pet alligator, named Robert E. Lee," said Mary. "He slept in a shoebox. He was my favorite, God rest his soul."

"What happened to Robert?"

"Robert E. Lee," she corrected. "Well, one January day, Robert E. Lee quit moving. Daddy buried him in the backyard. We had a funeral service and everything. I even wore a black armband to school."

Miss Mary shook her head. "I had no idea alligators hibernated in January."

ANNUAL EXAM

One of my friends is a vet. We were good friends as young men. We rooted for the same teams and even liked the same kinds of girls. Which was a big problem.

Because as it turns out, he was the attractive one.

And I was his opening act.

My buddy has more money than Benjamin Franklin. He graduated with a veterinary degree from a certain Alabama university – which shall remain nameless. He's a very successful vet, and I'm proud of him for earning nine times what I do.

But I'll admit, I'm even prouder when his college team loses.

I took Ellie Mae to my buddy for a check-up. I drove a long way just to see him. He ran his hands along Ellie's body, inspecting. Then, he patted her underbelly, examined her ears, and even inspected her tailpipe.

Ellie Mae growled.

Like any good Southern lady would.

After a few moments, my buddy came to a conclusion: Ellie Mae is fat.

I almost socked him in his cow-college kidneys.

"It's no big deal," he insisted. "Dogs gain weight. Just like people do. She needs to lay off the carbs."

"Carbs?"

He stroked Ellie's head. "She's the size of a horse. And large-breed dogs don't live long. Twelve years max. No more carbs."

I collapsed in the chair.

"It's not the end of the world," he said. "I'll hook you up, brother. I have some carb free food she's going to love."

"You do?"

"Absolutely," he said. "It's only seventy-two dollars per bag."

So, I bought six bags.

I can't have that fool thinking I'm poor.

RUN FORREST RUN

"Run Forrest!" the tour guide shouted.

I looked up from my book. Sure enough, I saw him. A man in a red Bubba Gump cap and Nikes – running. He sprinted through Chippewa Square like the Devil was after him. A tour bus of applauding people trailed behind.

"Look," the tour guide said. "It's Forrest Gump!"

When Forrest passed me, he bumped my sidewalk table. My hot coffee dumped right into my lap. It scalded me in a particularly sensitive region of my being.

A few minutes later, Forrest wandered back to me with his hat in his hands.

"Gosh," he said. "I'm sorry, I don't know what to say."

I stood up and shook his hand.

He sighed. "I've been performing this tour two years. That's never happened before. Can you forgive me?"

Of course I could.

Though my unborn children might not.

Forrest's real name is Ben. He's an actor from

Atlanta. He's been playing the part of Forrest Gump for tourists long enough to be sick of it. What Ben really wants is to leave Savannah and break into the Broadway scene. But that's easier said than done. He's already tried.

Three times.

"Uh oh." He looked at his wristwatch. "Another bus is coming. Quick," he said. "Smile and wave."

The bus rounded the corner. Ben flashed a smile and gave his best Forrest Gump wave.

"Look folks," the tour guide said. "There's Forrest Gump, he's chatting with a friend." The tour guide covered her mouth. "Oh my God, it looks like his friend has..."

"Pardon my friend." Forrest elbowed me. "He drank too much Dr. Pepper."

YOUNG MAN

Jamie loves visiting the grocery store. See, some folks go to the movies, or bowling. Not Jamie. On vacation, she slaps her lipstick on and goes to the nearest Publix.

I think what she enjoys most is giving employees a hard time. Especially awkward young men who are somewhat lazy and have pissy attitudes. Yesterday, one such young man was about to get a blessing. It all started when Jamie looked through the ice cream cooler. What she wanted was salted caramel ice cream, but all they had was vanilla. And Jamie would rather eat a day-old raccoon drumstick than vanilla ice cream.

"Excuse me, sir," she said to the Publix employee. "Do you have any more caramel ice cream in the back?"

He turned and gave her the same bewildered look your drunk aunt gives you when it's getting close to bedtime.

He shrugged his shoulders.

"What does that mean?" Jamie shot back.

"It means I don't know," said Herman Munster.

Jamie squinted her eyes at him. "Have you gone back to look?"

"Well, no."

"Oh, then you must have a long inventory list in that brain of yours?"

He shook his head.

"Hmmm, well that can only mean one thing." She crossed her arms.

"It can?"

"Sure, it means you have a fancy truck, and more money than Jesus Christ. And this job is something your momma made you do because you're too old to be sitting home playing video games. Furthermore, your truck is probably loud as $#!%."

"Yeah." I added. "With a killer stereo and superb gas mileage."

He shrugged. "It's not that superb."

THINK BEFORE YOU SPEAK

"You need to think before you speak," my friend's mother once told me.

That's code for: *you're a bigmouth.*

She was right. I had a bad habit of saying things. I used too many words, at too high of volume.

Too often.

I've always had a big mouth. I inherited it biologically from my mother. Mother and I are twins. We're unable to keep secrets, talk in low tones, or hold our liquor.

We also don't know a stranger.

I once watched Mother make friends with a homeless man at the grocery store. She struck up a conversation. Then, she bought him a pound of smoked pork, a bottle of orange juice, and gave him fifty dollars. They chatted for nearly an hour.

I think he enjoyed the conversation more than the food.

Additionally, Mother and I can't keep secrets. The expression is true: telephone, telegraph, tell-a-Dietrich.

One Christmas, my mother even revealed which presents she bought me. She warned me to keep it a secret.

But I told my father.

Then I told my Sunday school class.

And then my baseball team.

For the majority of my life, I've felt bad about my loudmouth. I wished I could be closed-lipped like some of my friends, but God didn't make me that way.

Mother once explained it to me in a way that I could grasp:

"Sean," she said. "Some people use brains, some people use popularity. But people like you use their voice. And there's a place for people like you."

Well, there's a place for people like you too.

Mother.

ONE-UPMANSHIP

I have a friend who's a terrible conversationalist, because of a certain bad habit. You might know the kind of person I'm talking about. My friend is a one-upper.

Here's how it goes:

If you wake up at six. He got up at four. If you exercise. He took second place in the Ironman. If it's one hundred degrees where you live, he lives on the equator. Anything you do, he does better. Anything you've done, he's done three times already.

It's mentally exhausting.

And it's not just him. I'll bet you have someone who one-ups you, too. One-uppers are everywhere.

Even the Walmart cashier has one-upped me. She noticed I was buying cholesterol-free butter. She smiled and said, "It's about time you cleaned up your diet." She went on to say, "I haven't eaten saturated fat since Ronald Regan."

How troubling.

I think saturated fat tastes good. Especially in the unique form of barbecued pork ribs.

Why must we one-up our fellow man like that? Why must folks insist on being the biggest, strongest, fastest, leanest, smartest, richest, and have the lowest blood pressure?

It's a rude way to behave. I believe we ought to let someone else be the biggest-smartest-richest for a change. The world would be a better place if we let others have preferential treatment. If we listened to each other, and said things like, "That's fascinating, tell me more."

Maybe one day, mankind will quit one-upping one another. And maybe then we'll all eat more barbecued pork ribs like we should.

My friend can join us.

He can eat twice as many ribs as you.

MY FRIEND'S MOM

As a young boy, my friend had a beautiful mother. We neighborhood boys thought she was the best thing since canned peaches. It might've been her long blonde hair, or her brown cow eyes. Either way, any of us would've gladly filled in for her husband.

My friend's mother was famous for more than just her looks. She was well-known for something we referred to as second-lunch. Which consisted of a Moon Pie and an RC Cola.

After eating lunch at our own houses, five of us neighborhood boys lined up on her back porch for second-lunch. Every day the same. And she'd make sure we left with full hands. Then, we'd sit beneath my friend's house and see how long we could make the meal last. Christopher could nibble on his Moon Pie for nearly an hour.

The longest mine ever lasted was thirty-two seconds.

One summer, we learned our friend's mother had cancer of the brain. At that age, none of us even knew what that was. It was aggressive. After only a few months, she lost her beloved hair, and she started speaking quieter. Most days, she stayed around her house, wearing a robe.

Several of us neighborhood boys came up with an idea to cheer her up. We gathered on her back porch like we used to. Single file. When she came to the door, we each handed her a Moon Pie and a greeting card.

She died a few weeks later.

And some of us haven't eaten Moon Pies since.

NINETY-ONE YEARS

I have an elderly friend who lives at The Magnolia House, in Quincy, Florida. She's ninety-one years old, and she's adopted me as her surrogate grandson. I go visit her from time to time. But not as often as either of us would like.

"You know," she said once. "Starting from birth, it takes twenty years to figure out who you really are."

"Twenty?" I said. "I wasn't even eating solid foods at twenty."

"It's true," she said. "When I was twenty, snap, I just knew."

"That easy?"

"Yep," she said. "But it does't end there. It took me another eighteen years to learn how to actually go for it."

"When you were thirty-eight?"

"Bingo."

Thirty-eight sounded reasonable.

"There's more," she explained. "It took twelve more years to work up the courage. See honey, knowing *how* to be yourself isn't enough. You have to be brave enough to do it."

I counted on my fingers. "So, you were fifty?"

"Yessir."

Ready or not fifty, here I come.

"I'm not done," she added. "It took me another twenty years not to give a damn what anyone else thought."

"Thought about what?"

"About being myself. It's one thing to be yourself. It's another not to care what folks think about it. Few will understand."

I counted again. "So, you were seventy?"

She winked. "Ah, but there's more. It took me fifteen more years to quit blaming people for not understanding."

I did more mental math. "Age eighty-five?"

She nodded.

"So," I said. "Let me get this straight. Eighty-five is when you *finally* found yourself?"

"Lord no," she said. "I don't even remember what the hell we're talking about."

TAR HEELS

It was two in the morning on Highway 87 when mother totaled our car. We were bound for Altamahaw, North Carolina when I saw a buck wander into the road. A Conway Twitty song played on the radio, and Mother's speedometer was clocking eighty-five when she hit him. I don't remember much after that, but I do remember shouting, "Mother!"

That's about all.

When I awoke, I was half-lying on the dashboard, covered in glass shards. My forehead was a mess. Mother's face was against the steering wheel, and my sister cried in the backseat. There wasn't a light around for miles and miles.

That's when he came.

It was too dark to make out his face, but I remember he was black, dressed in a Tar Heels T-shirt. He muscled the doors open, then removed each of us, one by one. He carried my limp mother over his shoulder and propped her up against a tree. Then, he came to me and said, "Hey Mister Sean, you're a strong little man aren't you?

Don't be scared by your own blood, now. You be strong for your momma, Sean."

He patted my shoulder.

And then he was gone.

It's been twenty-six years since that night. I've replayed it in my mind until I've almost worn out the record. No one knew who that man was, where he came from, or where he went. And for the life of me, I can't figure out how a perfect stranger, a Tar Heel, knew my first name.

But, I've always wanted to thank him.

Sometimes I do, before I fall asleep at night.

PEOPLE

I love people.

Big ones, small ones, young ones, and elderly ones. Especially the elderly ones. Also: tall people, short folk, skinny, normal-sized, smart, and mentally slow people. I think I like slow people best.

If you're simple enough to notice their wisdom, you'll find they're brilliant.

I also enjoy outdoorsmen – but I like outdoorswomen better. I like social-butterflies, wallflowers, homebodies, party-animals, and redheads. I love poets, singers, fishermen, talkers (like myself), thinkers, smokers, non-smokers, black folks, white folks, all the other skin colors, beer-drinkers, vodka-snobs, lesbians, gays, fry-cooks, butchers, bakers, and the proverbial candlestick makers.

Consequently, I made candles in the third grade. I used an old gym sock for the wicks, like the instructor suggested. Our house stunk for a week.

The truth is, I just love people. And I mean it. I like talking to them, I like understanding their approaches to life. I learn from them.

Well, at least I try to.

But, I haven't even mentioned the rotten people yet. I mean flat-out selfish folks. You know the ones. They're money-hungry, jealous, angry, grumpy, miserable, cocky, egocentric, or mad. They think of themselves first. They hate to pay for their own lunches, much less leave a good tip.

Sorry to say, I learn more from mean folks than I do nice people. They teach me about myself. I learn how good apples go bad. About how good people turn into angry ones, how integrity can be lost, how people can be cruel. Often times, I learn these folks don't even know what love is.

Well.

I love these people most of all.

GRANDADDY'S BUICK

My grandfather liked to give bits of quirky advice. While driving his Buick, he'd fling out nonsensical folk-sayings and leave me scratching my head. He'd say things like, "Don't go to sleep with your hair wet, you'll get a neck-ache." Another: "Blood is thicker than water, but molasses is thicker than blood, and peanut butter is thicker than molasses." It took me years to figure out what that meant. And then there's my personal Grandad-favorite, "Never touch stray dogs."

Never.

My grandfather would even go a step further and say, "When you're driving, don't swerve to avoid a stray dog in the road. You could flip your car." After saying that, he'd backup his claims with real-life examples. Stories about vehicles overturning on the highway, and people being barbecued alive in their Buicks.

All because of a stray mutt.

When Grandad drove me to Springdale, Arkansas, you can imagine my shock when a puppy trotted across the road. The thing pranced right in front of Grandad's ugly car. I covered my eyes and screamed, expecting him to plow over the innocent dog.

But he did not.

He slammed the brakes with both feet and muscled the wheel to one side. The car fishtailed in an S-pattern on the highway. When we finally screeched to a halt, Grandad hopped out and approached the puppy. It was black, with a tan chest. He squatted down and stroked its head. The puppy licked him once, so he named it Ronald. Ronald slept by Grandad's bed until his fur turned white.

And that's why we don't touch stray dogs.

THE ONLY THING I'VE EVER WON

When I was in sixth grade, Mrs. Doerkson, my teacher, submitted my work to the Regional Creative Writing Contest. They accepted me. And, I took first place in age-eleven category. It was the only thing I'd ever won, and Mrs. Doerkson was as proud as anyone on this planet. She took me out for ice cream thereafter.

Because Sean Dietrich loves ice cream.

Here is what sixth-grade-me had to say:

PRETTY GOOD SO FAR
By Sean Dietrich (Age 11)
Edited By Linda Doerkson

Life. I think I like life. It's been pretty good so far. I don't know what happens after we die, but it will probably be a lot like life. And why wouldn't it be? Life is the best thing ever made. What could be better than sunshine and trees and ice cream and grass and dogs and ice cream and oceans and girls and ice cream and poems and music?

Music. I think music is a little like life. You know what music does when you hear it? How it makes you think? When I hear it, I feel things I've only ever thought about.

Poems, I like them, too. But not as much as my daddy. He likes Robert Frost. He reads poetry out loud sometimes. I wish I understood poetry, but I don't. The words are too long. Daddy says I don't need to understand, but only to listen to the sounds of the words. He says poetry is not to be understood, but heard.

Maybe that's what life is like, too. Maybe life is the noises of words we can't understand. So, we just listen to the words, enjoying the way they feel in our ears. Kind of like music. Kind of like poetry.

Kind of like this.

NINETY-THREE DOLLARS AND FIFTY CENTS

The Walton County courthouse is a marvelous place to be during the afternoon. If you sit in one chair for more than a few minutes, you'll see interesting people pop through the double doors. You'll see boaters renewing tags, folks paying taxes, and of course, people buying marriage licenses.

I saw one such young couple.

"How was I supposed to know?" the young man said to his girlfriend. "I had no idea it cost so much to get married, I brought all the cash I had."

His girlfriend rubbed her extended belly. "You mean to tell me, we can't get married because you're short twenty-eight dollars?"

"And fifty cents," he added.

It was at this point I approached the happy couple. "Excuse me," I said. "I couldn't help but overhear." I dug my wallet out of my pocket. "I have twenty-six dollars here."

"Aww, dude," the man said. "Thanks, but I still need

two more dollars."

"And fifty cents," his girlfriend added.

So, I darted out to my truck and scavenged through my loose change. After ten minutes of digging, I came up with three dollars in quarters. I jogged back inside and plopped them into his hand.

The man hugged me.

"Do you want to be a witness for our wedding?" the girl asked.

Well, I'd never witnessed a courthouse wedding. It was a short ceremony. The county clerk even waived the extra fee as a wedding gift. The newlyweds kissed, then said a prayer while the clerk and I bowed our heads.

Let people say what they want about the world.

But I believe in love.

SATURDAY CARTOONS

Growing up, my television restrictions were lifted on Saturday mornings. It was like cotton-picking Christmas at the Dietrich's. I watched the same programs every blessed Saturday: Looney Tunes, Rocky and Bullwinkle, and Star Trek.

Always in that order.

On weekends, my mother worked and my father slept until ten. Before Daddy woke, I ate breakfast. Rice Krispies with sugar and whole milk. Extra sugar, extra milk, extra Krispies. Then, I'd clean my bowl and place it back in the cupboard.

I didn't want Daddy to know I'd eaten. I wanted him to think I was still hungry when he got up. Because if I was hungry, good things happened.

Namely, donuts.

The service station up the road had donuts. They weren't hot, and they tasted so-so, but they did just fine. Daddy would buy a dozen, along with coffee, and the paper. He'd make small-talk with the woman behind the counter, and I'd nearly die of starvation, waiting.

SEAN DIETRICH

When he finished chatting, we'd eat on the back of his tailgate, watching traffic whiz by. A few folks poked arms out of car windows when they passed. Others would pull over and have conversations. But then, some Saturdays, he'd sit and check the scores in the newspaper, and never say a single word.

Afterward, we'd return home and eat something inappropriate for lunch. Maybe root beer floats, or pancakes and Paydays.

I don't know why I'm telling you this. You couldn't possibly care about something so mundane. I suppose the older I get, the more I miss those Saturdays.

And I miss the one I spent them with.

RYAN

Ryan. That was my friend's name. He was at least two feet shorter than me. He was also light as a sack of rice cakes. So light, in fact, I could hold him over my head like a barbell.

Sometimes we performed for tips.

Ryan wasn't the same as ordinary people. He was slow, and he didn't have a typical outlook on life, either. The teachers called him "special," the hateful kids called him a "retard." We his friends, called him Spider-Man.

Ryan did his best to live up to that title.

Ryan's mother once explained why he was so unique. She said his umbilical cord wrapped around his neck in the womb. It slowed his development, and gave him lifelong heart problems. Well, all I can say is, God must've known what he was doing because Ryan turned out to be one of a kind.

Ryan loved country music. Loud. He also collected triple-peanut shells – the kind with three peanuts instead of two. He had bags full. Something else: he always walked as though he were perpetually falling forward. It was a unique march that seemed to announce, "Hey everybody, don't overlook me."

I remember the last time I saw Ryan, before his family moved away. I told Ryan I'd miss him, and that I would write him.

"Don't miss me," he said in his loud voice. "And don't write me, you know I hate to read."

"But Ryan, I like to write."

Ryan thought for a moment. "Then write something about me."

It's been twenty-three years.

This is that something.

NICE

What in the hell is Niceness? And where does it come from? What makes some people so bone-crushingly nice? I'm not talking about polite folks who say thank you and please. I'm talking about people who are so genial, so personable, so selfless and kind, they're super-human.

Nice.

Of course, here in the South, the word "nice" doesn't mean nice at all. It's Southern-speak for something much more serious. When a Southerner calls someone "nice," what they mean is: *This person is so generous, they deserve happiness, pretty babies, and their own book in the Bible.*

And it's true, these people deserve such things, because too few of them exist it seems. My guess would be, the percentage of nice people in the world – I'm practicing statistics without a license – is somewhere around six percent.

Maybe lower.

The truth is, I wish I were like these folks, but I'm

not. I often get grumpy when I don't have enough sleep. Which isn't nice. Nice people don't do that. They don't get cranky. Not ever. Not even if they've been awake for three days straight, have a broken ankle, and an incurable case of the Egyptian yellow fever.

I don't know what makes these people tick. They have the same problems I have, they sit through the same traffic jams I do, and they pay the same property taxes I pay. But they're not bitter about it. They'll give you anything they own, even money from their pockets. And they'll do it in a way that won't make you feel ashamed, but inspired. They're just nice.

They make me want to get more sleep.

So I can be nice too.

THE HEREAFTER

Like anyone else, I've thought about the afterlife since I was knee-high to an iPhone. But thinking about the afterlife doesn't make me any more certain about what happens. Though sometimes it feels good to wonder about it.

I know some people believe we come back again. Could that be true? What if I come back as a cricket, or worse, a poop fly? A tiny invertebrate with no other charter in life but to loiter around cattle pastures and swim freestyle in mugs of morning coffee.

Other folks think we dematerialize into something like dirt. Will I become a pile of fine dust? Will I lay on the ground like a violated jar of Cajun seasoning powder? Will they build something on top of my soil in the future century? Say, a strip mall, or a sewage processing facility?

You know what I think happens when we finally kick the oxygen habit? I'll tell you what I think. But first, I should admit that this is not my own theory. This particular speculation belongs to a five-year-old named

Angie. I once asked Angie what she thought happened when we're finally taken out of production.

"I know what happens," she said.

"You do?"

"Yes." She didn't even have to think about it.

"What happens?"

"Something so good!" She jumped once. "We won't have to clean our rooms anymore. We'll eat chocolate whenever we want, and watch movies. And bad people will be small." She squinted through her pinched fingers. "This small. See?"

Yes Angie.

I think I do see.

EGOCENTRIC

Long ago, in a college psychology class, the instructor told us our egos were good things. Something our brain uses to protect us, to save our precious self-esteem. It almost makes sense, but I don't buy it. I can't recall a single instance my self-righteous ego ever stepped in to save the day.

Quite the opposite.

Like anyone else, I have a healthy ego. Sometimes it comes out to play, even though I wish it would stay underneath its ugly rock. Like the time when I was sixteen. Tara Roseman told me I had a hawk-nose. "I most certainly do not," I said. "I just happen to breathe more air than other people." And then I walked home without her.

Another time: I was fired from a job for something I didn't do. So, I placed a block of bleu cheese in the air conditioning vent of the manager's office. The smell got so bad they called an exterminator.

And I'm only picking soft examples. My ego has been worse than that. Much, much worse. Consider the time I felt wronged by someone who was important to me. My ego did the worst thing it could've done. It clamped my mouth shut, it made me withdraw. I went months without talking to this person. Months grew into years. I didn't answer the phone, I even threw away letters without ever opening them.

That person died a few years ago.

She was survived by a husband and two good-looking kids. And I was too concerned with my own life to even know about it.

And it stings my ego to admit that.

SICK TO HER STOMACH

My mother-in-law poured a Collins glass of bourbon and then splashed a faint whisper of Coca-Cola in it. She did it simply so she could call it a bourbon and Coke, which sounds more ladylike than say, double bourbon.

"Did I ever tell you about my stomach problem?" Miss Mary asked.

"No ma'am."

"Well, I had a stomach issue when I was a girl, I couldn't keep food down." Mary took a sip, then coughed. "Wow, that's strong."

Don't look at me, Mary, I didn't make it.

She went on, "The doctor tried to get me to eat chicken and dumplings, but I didn't want them."

"No dumplings?" I said. "It'll be a December day in Hell if I ever thumb my nose up at a dumpling."

"They tried to get me to eat soup," she said. "Tomato, cream of mushroom, beef, even raccoon stew."

"Coon?"

"Yep. Lots of folks in Brewton ate coon. Jessie Mae would keep a coon in a pen two weeks before she killed and cooked it."

How nice.

"Mother also tried to get me to drink warm milk, orange juice, and tomato juice. I couldn't keep anything down. Doctor said if I didn't eat something soon, I'd waste away."

"So what'd you do?"

"It was Daddy," she said. "He saved the day. He gave me whiskey. After one shot, I'd feel so giddy, I'd eat anything."

"Are you pulling my leg?"

"Hand to God." She crossed her heart. "I drank one shot every night. They called it medicine. It's the only thing that kept me alive."

"So what happened?"

Mary took another sip. "I never got better."

CAKE AND ICE CREAM

September 11, 1994, was the night my father turned forty-one. His forty-first birthday was perhaps the most memorable night of my life.

It was a grand party. We even grilled steaks, and we never did that. Mother also made a huge cake, five layers, topped with white frosting, made to feed an army of guests. She let me help decorate it. On the top, Mother spelled out, "Forty-one, the beginning of the end" in blue icing.

Her version of a joke.

Everyone ate outside on the porch while the sun went down. When supper ended, Mother and I presented the cake. Everybody sang a chorus of "Happy Birthday," I tagged the melody with my usual operatic, "and many more."

My father laughed at the blue text on the cake, then ate two pieces, along with three bowls of ice cream. I remember this very clearly, because I did the same thing.

After eating so much in one sitting, everyone started getting sleepy. At eight-thirty, folks shook hands and left for home. We watched their red taillights disappear down our one-thousand-foot red dirt driveway. Then, my father and I sat by the pond and watched the stars come out. He pointed out the Big Dipper, but he was several constellations off.

I didn't bother to correct him.

After our hindparts got sore from sitting, we hiked up to the house. Mother was already in bed. We ate one more slice of cake. And by then, the cake was demolished. You couldn't even see the iced blue lettering anymore. He died forty eight hours later.

And all I can remember are those damned blue letters.

WEATHERMEN

"What do you want to be when you grow up?" I asked my nephew.

He wasn't sure. He closed his eyes tight. "I don't know," he said. "Maybe a therapist?"

My mother-in-law joined our conversation. "What about an astronaut?" she suggested. "I remember a time when all little boys wanted to be astronauts."

"Or weathermen," I added.

Mary wrinkled up her face. "No. A weatherman? That's just ridiculous."

I didn't see what was so silly. "Hey, I've always wanted to be a television meteorologist. If it wasn't for all the hard work and science, that's probably what I'd be."

"It's not a practical profession," she said. "I don't think I've ever met a single weatherman. Certainly never in Brewton."

"But Miss Mary, how many astronauts have you met in Brewton? Space travel is the most impractical profession there is. There're a lot more weathermen in the world than there are astronauts."

"Yeah," my nephew agreed, picking his nose.

"But astronauts," Miss Mary explained. "Are part of the United States Army. It's a good government job, it's part of the Constitution."

"Constitution?" I said.

My nephew imitated me. "Consticktooshoes?"

"Miss Mary," I said. "Being an astronaut isn't part of the Constitution. Our founding fathers didn't even know what space travel was."

"Fine then," Miss Mary answered with a little piss and vinegar in her voice. "But they didn't know anything about the weather back then, either."

"Yeah," my nephew stuck his tongue out at me.

"Hey," I said to him. "I thought you were on my side."

"I'm not on anybody's side," he said. "I'm a therapist, remember?"

TRAVELS WITH MARY

Traveling with Jamie's mother is a treasured experience.

The thing about mother-in-laws is they have needs. Lots of needs. And their needs rank higher than yours. It's only right. Try to remember, they've been alive longer than you. Long enough to have grown particular about these needs. Everything must be done in a specific way.

Even breakfast.

Look, I know you consider dried cereal to be a suitable breakfast. Most people do. But unless your mother-in-law is completing a federal prison sentence, Raisin Bran will not do. No way, nohow. She prefers you to rustle up three eggs, sausage, grits, bacon, and a glass of Alka-Seltzer. And please, be careful not to make the coffee too strong. It must be weak enough so that it's the color of watered down scotch.

Something else to remember: schedules. They aren't set in stone. Never. Schedules should be mysterious, and fun. Try removing your wristwatch and sliding it into your pocket. You won't need it anymore. Being on time only takes the magic out of life.

Another important thing to keep in mind while traveling: mother-in-laws have teacup-sized bladders. It's not their fault. They come from the factory that way. But no need to worry, this is rarely an issue. Unless, of course, your mother-in-law sips a Big-Gulp sweet tea during your seven-hour car ride. In that case, you'll want to look for cattle pastures off desolate Highway 10. When you escort her up to that old oak tree, make sure you bring her cane along.

Then, turn your back to her.

Plug your ears and sing Amazing Grace.

ASPIRATIONS

"You lack ambition," a past girlfriend once told me. "You're dragging me down."

Huh? I didn't know what the girl was talking about. What could be more ambitious than spending eleven whole years in junior college?

"And buy a new truck," she said. "That thing's hideous." Then she shut the door and bid me goodnight.

My truck? That thing was a classic. With two hundred eighty thousand miles on the odometer and a bumper made from a two-by-four, it was a rusty charm-wagon.

But, she had a point. Compared to some people, I didn't have the ambition God gave a lap dog. I wish I could tell you I'm more ambitious nowadays, but I'm not. I don't want to climb to the next level – whatever that means – I'm not even sure I like the level I'm at now. In fact, I prefer to be a few notches lower.

Don't get me wrong, it's not that I don't care; I do. I have life-aspirations. They just look bad on paper.

Here's one: I like chocolate cake donuts. Right this

moment, I aspire to eat two, with coffee. Afterward, I aspire to take an emergency blood sugar nap. When I awaken, I aspire to watch Casablanca for the eight-thousandth time, and think about filing another extension on my taxes. Maybe not today, maybe not tomorrow. But soon.

Later tonight, maybe I will aspire to take my hideous truck to the beach, maybe do some fishing and watch a sunset.

I know this kind of ambition doesn't really count.

But I can promise you, it's more fun than junior college.

MINUET IN G

In all my life, I've only taught one person how to play the piano. Jillian. She was ten years old, three-foot tall, with coal black hair. She lived in the apartment next to ours.

When I first met Jillian, she was wrestling in the breezeway with her younger brother. She beat the tar out of him using a stuffed animal. I introduced myself, but Jillian acted like she didn't hear me.

Because Jillian was deaf.

I'm not sure why that little girl was so hellbent on learning the piano, but she was mesmerized by the upright in my den. One day, she signed something to me. Her brother translated, "Jillian wants you to teach her piano."

I told Jillian it wasn't a good idea.

Jillian signed a circular, "please," on her chest. Her face was as serious as the dark side of the moon.

So, I gave in. I tried to teach Jillian to count in rhythm, and then demonstrated hand positions. It took a few months of irregular practice. Eventually, she could eek through a simplified version of "Minuet in G" while I tapped count for her. She was terrible.

Sometimes, after playing she'd make hand motions to her brother.

He'd respond with, "It sounds great Jilly."

I remember the day Jillian's family moved out of the building. She and her brother came to say goodbye. Then, Jillian played on my piano one last time, just the way I'd instructed her. Her playing was out of rhythm, and she hit a river of wrong notes. It sounded God-awful.

But it was the prettiest damn music I've ever heard.

BUY ME A BEER

"Hey you," the little old black man said. "You from out of town?"

"Me?" I asked. "Yessir, I am."

"Look, if you buy me a beer, I'll tell you all about Savannah. I'm a local, I've lived here all my life."

It sounded like a reasonable offer. And he looked like he hadn't eaten in a few days. I bought him a beer, along with a hamburger, fries, conch fritters, and a slice of cheesecake. In return, he told me all about the old city – in his own words.

"You see," he began. "Savannah was founded by Colonel Sanders and Jimmy Carter in the year 1982."

"Huh?"

"Yessir." He crammed a handful of fries into his mouth. "Little known fact, president Garth Brooks built this bar we're sitting at. With his own bare hands."

"President Garth Brooks?" I exchanged looks with the bartender.

"Quiet," the man scolded me. "Let me finish, there's more. A famous book was written in this city, too."

"I know," I said. *Midnight in the Garden of Good and Evil.*

"Nope," he said. "The last book of the Bible." He took a big bite of his hamburger. "Benjamin Franklin wrote that other book you're talking about."

My mistake.

After he finished eating, the gentleman and I went outside. I had to help him stand up straight, but his guided tour wasn't over. Not yet. He showed me where Simon met Garfunkle, and the street corner where Elvis discovered the theory of electricity.

Then, he robbed me of all my cash.

And I pretended to be upset about it.

INVISIBLE BOYS

No dialogue about my life would be complete without discussing some of my experiences with the opposite sex. I'll go all the way back, and start there. Beginning with Courtney Lackman:

Courtney Lackman had been my steady girl since kindergarten. By the fourth grade she was an awkward gangly ten-year-old with a large head and mile-long arms. Her blonde hair was wiry, and her eyes were about the size of billiard balls. Some boys called her, Ugly Puggly Lackman – possibly the most uncreative nickname to ever hit the fourth grade, but you get the idea.

However.

One singular summer changed everything for Courtney. When we all returned to school, still sporting our summer tans and fake fishing stories, something was different about her. Seemingly overnight, Courtney Lackman had become the most popular thing to ever happen to a blouse. And it made her a smash with the boys. And, as these things go, her newfound popularity gave way to a sudden disinterest in me.

I was crushed. I felt ugly and invisible at the same time. I needed to prove myself to Courtney. So, I did what all boys my age did when they wanted to prove something; I signed up for the football try-outs.

Try-outs were held on the high-school football field. And during the auditions, a handful of girls would position themselves on the bleachers like spectators at the Kentucky Derby. There, they would select which boys would be eligible bachelors, and which boys would be sentenced to play trombone in the middle-school band. They peered down at the us boys with flat-faced smiles, notepads in laps.

"Suit up boys," the coach called out. "We're going to see what the hell God made you titty-babies out of."

Bobby Ryder helped this titty-baby attach the rank smelling high-school equipment to my chubby frame. He cinched the straps around my chest, then handed me a g-string with a cup-shaped device. "Here, wear this," Bobby said. "It's for your – you know – just make sure it's really on there good."

It looked like something meant to cradle a sleeping toddler. "Bobby, do they have anything a little smaller?"

"Nope, you'll have to make do, now hurry up, big boy."

I bumbled the thing over my eighth-grade unmentionables, then walked onto the field the same way John Wayne might walk after an all-night ride across the Sierra.

Coach Updyke stood with a football in his hands, his bushy eyebrows forming a straight line across his forehead. He stared at us like he was already disappointed in our poor genetics. And I suppose he had reason to be. If he would've tallied up all our combined weights, we football hopefuls might've tipped the scales at a buck-fifty, sopping wet, with pockets full of sand and gravel.

I looked at my comrades, who wore the same oversized helmets, and tight-fitting polyester pants I wore. Each one of us, acutely aware of the sundresses perched in the bleachers.

"Okay," Coach shouted. "You four, over there, you four on the other side. Hop to it!"

We did as we were told, hobble-running like dwarfs carrying pumpkins between our legs. Four of us stood shoulder to shoulder, facing our peers.

"Alright!" the coach hollered. "Now tackle the holy Jesus out of each other!"

I stood motionless, blinking. The truth was, I didn't know how to squeeze the "holy Jesus" out of a grapefruit, let alone someone my own age.

"Go on!" the coach shouted again. "You heard me you panty-wearing titty-babies, knock each other down!"

That was all Roddy Sounder needed to hear. Roddy powered into me with everything he had. The titty-baby somersaulted backward, then crashed onto the ground like a busted brick.

"That was good, Roddy," said Coach. "Now that right there, boys, is what football looks like."

I limped to my feet. My groin protector had become dislodged, creeping down my leg like a turtle late for an appointment.

"Get in your positions!" Coach Updyke popped my rear end with a towel. "Let's try it again!"

Four of us stumbled to the line and assumed our crouching stances. I glanced at Courtney Lackman sitting in the bleachers. She didn't even acknowledge me. Such cold prepubescent female judgement is enough to land a man in therapy for the rest of his life.

The coach's whistle screeched. Before I could figure out which way was east, Roddy plowed into me like forty-mule-team Borax. This time the wind was knocked clean out of me. I laid inert on the grass, unable to breathe, suspended between real-life and Purgatory.

"Get up!" Coach yelled to me.

But it was too late, half of me had already gone to be with Jesus.

Aggravated, Coach Updyke walked over to me. He tugged the belt of my hosiery upward, joggling me like a collection of jingle-bells. It's a maneuver practiced on football fields across America. And I've never understood how such a technique helps unfortunate titty-babies regain their dignity.

"Come on now, boy," he sounded like Charlton Heston. "Breathe dammit, breathe."

I did *not* breathe. Dammit. I could only flop.

Coach dropped me and shook his head. "Somebody get this titty-baby off the field."

But, my fifth-grade constituents were unable to lift the titty-baby off the ground. So each boy took one of Titty-Baby's legs and dragged him across the turf on his itty-bitty titty-baby back.

"You going to make it?" Bobby asked me, propping me up against the fence. His voice seemed to come from the sky.

"No," I said. "Just go on without me."

"Aw, cheer up, you'll be fine. Now tell me your name, so I know you're okay."

I did not answer such a dumb question. Bobby had known me since preschool, he already knew my name.

"I'm not leaving," he said. "Not until you can say your name and prove you're alive."

"Courtney Lackman," I moaned.

"You wish."

When try-outs were over, the coach told everyone on the field to take a knee. I wasn't able to do that, but I was able lay flat on my back just fine.

The coach read the results of the audition aloud. Girls in the bleachers tapped their pencil leads on their tongues, ready to make notes. Coach read through the entire list without ever once saying my name – except to say, "someone flip that boy over onto his stomach so he doesn't choke on his own vomit."

I didn't make the team.

I did, however, manage to break my tailbone, and I suppose that counts for something. The doctor told me my coccyx would likely heal itself within six weeks to fifty years. He was right. To this day, I can predict cold fronts by a dull pain that radiates from the area where the Good Lord split me.

Needless to say, I never played organized football again. The only exception being, at family gatherings, when Uncle Frank attempts to demonstrate that herniated discs "don't mean shit."

Well, they most certainly do.

It should be understood: in the town I grew up in, there are two kinds of boys. There are those who play football, and those who bake cookies with their grandmother. If you don't play football, you might as well sign up for the drama department and start wearing a scarf. Because, to the local female persuasion, you're about as useful as buttons on a dishrag.

Since Courtney Lackman wanted nothing to do with a boy with a "broken little ass-bone," who baked oatmeal raisins every Saturday night with Gram Gram, she chose to wholly ignore me from then on. And that was the end of what should've been our lifelong romance. I mourned her loss, because she was more than a girl to me. She was my friend.

Fifth-grade was getting off to a great start.

I'd be lying if I didn't tell you I started to resent Courtney. I went from loving the ground she walked on to despising her.

Each time I'd see her hook arms with another boy, I'd curl my upper lip in a half-snarl. I tried not to think about the time Courtney kissed me underneath her mother's bed when we were five. "You taste like Pledge furniture polish," she told me then. Little did she know, I'd been practicing kissing on my mother's end tables.

The newly developed Courtney rarely said anything more to me than "hello," or, "you're standing in my way, piss stain."

But then came etiquette class.

In our middle school, the class was mandatory for a all students. It was a class, designed to teach children the importance of using the right fork at a dinner party; how to fold a napkin; and how to refrain from slurping soup like a caged feral pig. The whole operation was presided over by a woman with a beehived hair-do named, Miss Carrie.

Miss Carrie was as uptight as any self-respecting church organist ought to be. She rolled her R's when she spoke, and resented all boys for having extra Y chromosomes. Some of the boys called her Scary Carrie, or Harry Carrie – depending on the boy's preference. And, in turn Miss Carrie gave us all F's. None of us boys cared what we made in etiquette class anyway, except for Tyler Murphy, who still peed sitting down. A habit I'd abandoned long ago, per my mother's urging.

The graduation dinner was a belittling ceremony indeed, in which boys and girls donned their Sunday best, then suffered through an adult dinner party together – minus the lubrication of alcohol. Parents attended our supper, though I'm not sure why. Benevolent mothers went to great pains preparing mountains of wonderful casserole dishes. And because of that, it was the best day of the year. The day we stuffed ourselves tighter than ticks with cheese potato casserole and sour cream dip.

On the day of class graduation, Courtney wore a black velvety dress her mother had ordered from a catalog. To this day, I don't think I've seen a dress more striking. And, as the Good Lord would have it, Courtney Lackman was assigned to be my partner.

Our first date.

Never before had I stumbled into such opportunity. But my luck didn't last for long. My attitude of hopefulness turned sour when I caught Courtney making goo goo eyes at Lee Carson across the room. That idiot even blew her a kiss. It was an affront to the very fibers of my masculinity.

When I saw that, I became indignant toward the rest of the world. My general demeanor degraded from moderately happy, to downright piss-poor.

It went like this:

"Okay class," said Miss Scary. "We're walking with our dates, arm in arm, like ladies and gentleman."

And we obeyed.

"Good, good," Miss Scary narrated. "That's it, proud members of upper-society, with bright futures, and lots of promise."

Mozart's Requiem played on Miss Scary's turntable, while we marched like a funeral procession of Lords and Duchesses.

"Now," Miss Scary said, waving her hands to the music. "We're walking to our assigned seats at our tables, looking for our place-cards, remembering to move with elegance. Nice recovery Kristen, walking in heels can be very difficult. Keep your head up John. Tuck in your shirt tail Phillip or I'll string you up by your elbows and gut you, ass first."

We all located our place-cards, and stood behind our chairs, arm in arm with our dates.

"Boys," Miss Scary said. "Slide the chairs outward for your ladies, allow them to sit."

I pulled Courtney's chair out.

Courtney mumbled, "Let's get this over with, titty-baby. I don't want to be seen with you."

"I'm not a titty-baby," I whispered back. "You're a hussy."

"You're the biggest titty-baby I've ever seen."

"Ladies," Miss Scary said, motioning to the room. "Take your seat in, and don't forget to thank the gentlemen for their chivalry."

Chivalry my ass. When Courtney went to sit down, I yanked the chair backward from underneath her. Her rear hit the floor like a sack of Emily Post books.

Courtney yelped.

Miss Scary killed the music, and ran to attend. "Courtney, are you alright? Speak to me. Speak to me child."

Where was Miss Scary during my football try-outs?

By some bizarre twist of fate, if you can believe it, Courtney had broken her tailbone. I hated myself for doing such a thing to Courtney Lackman, who really didn't do anything wrong at all. The truth was, I would've rather died than inflict pain on her. I just wanted her to notice me. I just wanted to be important to her again.

Years later, I sent Courtney a letter that read:

> Dear Courtney, I feel bad about everything that went on between us. I hope you'll see fit to forgive me. I'm sorry I called you a hussy. And I'm sorry I broke your tailbone.

She sent me a card back.

> Sean, I'm sorry you broke your tailbone, too.

And she never spoke to this titty-baby again.

OLD MAN IN A ROCKER

God Almighty has turned a deaf ear to me on many, many occasions. He's good at doing that. In Heaven, any envelopes marked with my address on them are thrown into the "return" pile.

The Old Man sits up there, in his rocking chair way up in the sky. That big cloud of Marlboro smoke you see wafting around him are my ubiquitous prayers. He fans most them away from his face like offensive diesel fumes.

I suppose it's for good reason. Because if the Old Man had answered every prayer I've ever prayed there's no telling what kind of mess my life would be in. I'd likely be living in the mountainous part of North Carolina, eating yellow snow, stealing drinking water from my neighbor's garden hose. Instead, I live in Florida, I enjoy my work, I eat what I want for breakfast, and I never eat yellow snow unless it comes from a snow-cone dispensary.

Like anyone else, I've made a lot of foolish prayers. I've prayed for things I thought I wanted, for people I thought loved me, for money, for baseball teams to win, for success. I've also made a great many prayers when the proverbial fertilizer has hit the fan, asking to be bailed out of tight spots.

Statistically, I'd say only two-percent of my prayers have ever been answered. Those are staggeringly terrible odds, considering the amount of prayers I've submitted. However, a few of my prayers have actually been answered immediately, and I'll never forget those.

Here are a few:

One hot July day, during a Little League game. The Bonner Springs Tigers were beating us like used bongo drums. I dropped to a knee and asked the Almighty for a grand-slam home run, in the bottom of the ninth inning.

To my surprise, He answered me. Instantaneously. However, He made a slight oversight. Instead of granting the home run to me, he gave the privilege to my teammate Phillip, who is as arrogant as the French nation. Old Phillip smacked that ball so hard, it sounded like a shotgun blast. The crowd tore the place apart, celebrating Phillip as a town hero.

Phillip gloats about that event to this very day. If you buy him a few drinks, he'll gloat about a few other things, too. And eventually he'll want to arm wrestle some poor idiot at the bar. You'll probably have to drive

Phillip home.

Another prayer answered: A very large man in a bar outside Chiefland, Florida once threatened to, "kick my ass backward, forward, and inside-out." I'd never seen an ass kicked inside-out before, so I prayed God would keep my ass outside-out. The man beat the tar out of me. When I asked a friend what my ass looked like, he answered with, "It looks like it's been dipped in turpentine and lit with a match."

"Thank God," I said. "I was afraid you were going to tell me it was inside-out."

Another miraculous prayer answered: at the movie theater, when I lost my jacket. The pimple-faced boy behind the lost and found counter refused to let me have my coat back. The boy said it was a very fine jacket, and he was unsure whether I was the original owner. He went on to say he'd be glad to let me have it for a nominal fee.

"The real owner of this coat," said the boy. "Would be happy to pay forty dollars for it, since it must've cost several hundred dollars."

"But, this is lost and found. You're supposed to just hand it over to me."

He touched the leather. "It's a *very* lovely coat."

"That was a gift, you greasy prick."

"Greasy prick? Sixty dollars."

I was so angry, I did a terrible thing. I prayed silently for God to strike the boy down, preferably with a dramatic flash of lightning and a voice from the sky. Then, I dug into my wallet, handed him three twenty-dollar bills, and thanked him for not letting his Christian charity stand in the way of his ignorance.

Much to my surprise, no sooner had the boy handed me the jacket, than he fell to the ground like a brick.

My heart stopped. Right then and there, I dropped to my knees and prayed for three parcels of beachfront property.

As it turned out, the boy only had a foot cramp brought on by severe dehydration, and I never inherited so much as a sea oat.

Yet another instance: once, while driving from Alabama to North Carolina, I came upon a deer on the side of the road. The deer had been hit by a car, and all it could do was lay there. I prayed God would help the poor animal, to ease its suffering. I even shed a few tears.

With that, the deer leapt to its feet and charged me with its antlers. It tore through my clothes and left me with a six-inch cut on my abdomen. The deer limped away into the woods grunting at me. I tell people my scar comes from a fist fight in Chiefland, where I successfully "turned some fella's ass inside-out."

Here's another one: while staying at a cabin high in the Georgia foothills, for Thanksgiving, one of the hickory logs in the fireplace let out a loud pop. It sent sparks into the den and set the rug on fire. The first thing I did was shout, "Jesus Christ, somebody get me some goddamn water!" It wasn't really a prayer, but nonetheless, my wife showed up in the living room carrying a glass of water saying, "No need to get grumpy, I've warned you about staying hydrated in this cold dry weather."

Here's an answered childhood prayer: once, many

years ago, I asked the Almighty for money to attend the youth group canoe trip. The canoe trip was an annual gallivant to ride aluminum canoes down a river. Everyone who was worth their salt was going on the trip. That is, everyone except one chubby little boy with the outside-out ass. So, I took to raising funds through innovative means, and I asked the Lord Jesus Christ to aid me in my efforts.

Texas Hold'em was the game. I'd bought a trick deck of cards from the back of *Popular Mechanics Magazine.*

One night, after Wednesday evening service, behind the church, I managed to rack up almost two hundred dollars. The pastor caught wind of my activities. He called me into his office, sat me down and shook his head at me. "Where," he said, "in the name of Moses did you get that deck of cards? And where can I get one?"

The truth is, I realize the Old Guy has been doing me a favor by withholding the things I thought I needed. I see that now. If He would've granted all my adolescent whims, my heart would be rotten to the core like one of those spoiled brats on reality television shows, which is anything but reality – unless you call living in a mansion with fifty blondes all clawing each other for the chance to jump in your bed reality.

Getting what I want would only cause me to forget about my fellow man. Those who are out of work. People who are hungry. The woman with auburn hair by the supermarket stoplight, holding a handwritten sign that read, "Mother of three, anything helps."

I wish I had more to give that woman.

I'll be honest, I'm glad God hasn't answered my

selfish prayers – hard as that is to admit. I'm even grateful for it. After all, the world doesn't need another man with a yacht, folding paper airplanes out of hundred-dollar bills, throwing them at women in red pumps.

Because quite frankly, that sounds miserable.

ME IN MY OWN WORDS

As a child, I liked to write. I filled up notebooks with tales of the high-seas, shameless vixens, and steamy scenarios combining both of the aforementioned. My fifth grade teacher found one of my notebooks and scanned through it. She told me I wrote with too many commas, and encouraged me to pursue a career in construction work.

That, old, woman, never, liked, me.

Years later, I learned my teacher had left the school. She took a job at the Piggly Wiggly as a cashier. I went to visit the old girl, to show her the man I'd grown into.

She seemed genuinely glad to see me. And I was just as glad to find her wearing that red apron for a living. After visiting for a few minutes, I realized something I'd never noticed before. Beneath her hardshell exterior was a regular lady, working from nine to five for pennies. She was doing the best she could with her life. Just like me.

Before I left, she asked me what kind of work I did.

At the time, I worked in construction.

SEAN DIETRICH

Sean Dietrich is a writer, humorist, and novelist, known for his commentary on life in the American South. His humor and short fiction appear in various publications throughout the Southeast, including South Magazine, *the* Tallahassee Democrat, Wired Magazine, Food Network Blog, Outdoors Magazine, *and he is a member of the NWU. His first short story was published during childhood, in a hometown journal newspaper. Since then, he's pursued his literary interests authoring four novels, writing humor, and short stories.*

An avid sailor and fisherman, when he's not writing, he spends much of his time aboard his sailboat (The S.S. Squirrel), *riding the Gulf of Mexico, trying not to die, along with his coonhound, Ellie Mae.*

FOR MORE STORIES, OR TO CONTACT SEAN, VISIT:
WWW.SEANDIETRICH.COM